Mommy is Effing Tired

by **Dr. Amenze Osa**

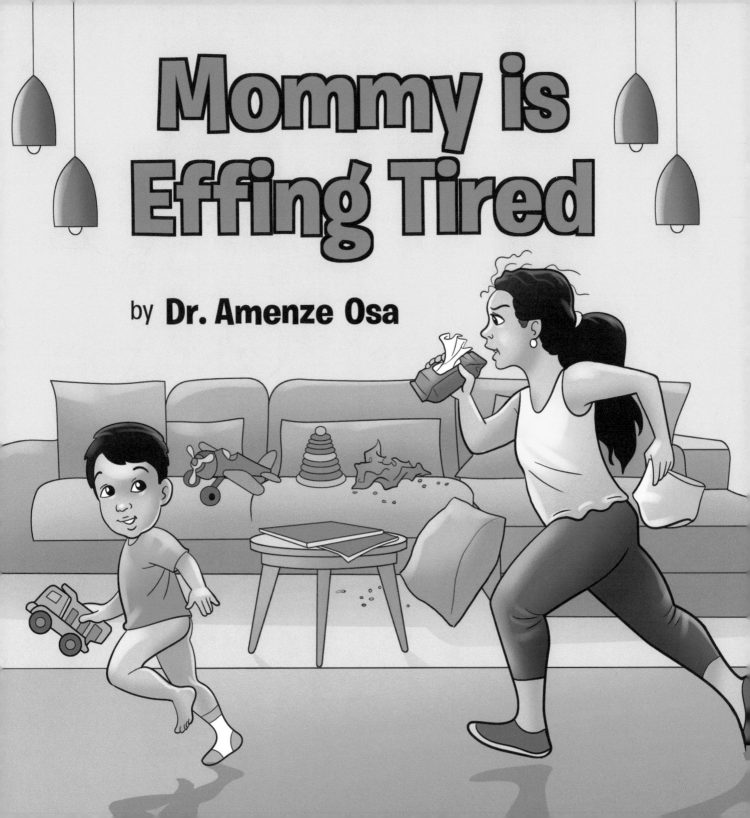

To my daughter, Ofy, and any other children
who will make this mommy and all other mommies effing
tired. Know that love is an action that takes work, energy,
and time --and someone loves you to
the point of exhaustion and beyond.

Also, thank you to my family members and the many dear
friends (both in person and online in my mom groups)
who encouraged me and helped make this book possible.

Weekend dishes to do
and laundry to fold.

But you won't eat your breakfast
and your food is now cold.

Mommy is effing tired!

I'd love to work out
and strengthen my body.

But your diaper needs changing,
or you just missed the potty.

Ugh! Mommy is effing tired!

I should clean the bathroom,
but you won't take your nap.

And you're screaming quite loudly
for another snack.

Hey! Mommy is effing tired!

Your toys are all over.
They cover the floor.

I've no time to check emails.
I just keep getting more.

Mommy is really effing tired!

The groceries are here,
but I'm too tired to cook.

So I order a pizza
and try reading you a book.

Because Mommy is effing tired!

You've run through the house,
avoiding your bath.

But I catch you and make sure
you're clean at last.

Mommy is effing tired!

Bedtime is a chore.
It's time for lights out.

You do need your rest
even if you must pout.

Please! Mommy is effing tired!

Soon you give into sleep
and you're dreaming at last.

But Mommy's too tired
to tackle her list of tasks.

It's literally only 9pm,
but Mommy is effing tired!

Being Mommy is hard,
and some days aren't as fun.

But there's no doubt about it—
through it all, I love you tons.

So remember that Mommy
has so much to do.

Try your best to be good
and know that Mommy always loves you.

Still... I'm... So. Effing. Tired!

Meet
Dr. Amenze Osa

Dr. Amenze Osa is a mom, wife, daughter, sister, friend, and eye surgeon. She started this book as a cathartic note in her phone, a stressed and fatigued new mom and surgeon, furloughed in 2020 due to the health pandemic.

So she wrote the beginnings of this book and eventually had the idea to put it out into the world for other moms who are taking on the stressful, but rewarding, job of mom. Moms who've been there and moms who are there. A quick and satisfying read that lets the mommies of the world know— somebody else is effing tired, too, and we'll get through this exhausting and amazing thing called motherhood together.

 @osa.eye.md
@mommy.is.effing.tired